*Reuel Jubilee presents:*

# Thoughts Guided by Truth

*Poetry to aid you along your spiritual journey through the collective mind.*

## The House of Jubilation Book

*Reuel Jubilee presents:*

*Thoughts Guided by Truth*

Published by:

## The House of Jubilation LLC

Detroit, Michigan

Copyright © 2024 by Reuel Richardson

All rights reserved

*No part of this book may be reproduced in any form, by photostat, microfilm, xerography, or any other means, or incorporated into any information retrieval system, electronic or mechanical, without the written permission of the copyright owner.*

# Founders Pillar

Dear Honored Supporter,

Thank you for your contribution to the progression of The House of Jubilation LLC. In this foundational stage of our unique publishing company, your donation is pivotal to the longevity of this ambitious endeavor. Our mission is to create and nurture safe spaces where individuals can engage deeply with transformative art, fostering reflection, connection, and enlightenment.

At The House of Jubilation, we envision a world where art, literature, and music inspire profound reflection, foster connection, and elevate consciousness. We aim to be a leading publisher that empowers creators to share transformative works, enriching the human experience and cultivating communities that thrive on creative expression, wisdom, and unity.

We value Communion, Education, Creative Expression, and the Application of Knowledge. We prioritize fostering meaningful connections and shared experiences through art. We believe in the power of learning and seek to offer knowledge that informs and inspires. We celebrate and encourage the freedom to express and explore the full range of human creativity. We emphasize the practical application of knowledge, transforming it into wisdom that enhances both individual and collective growth.

    This copy of *Reuel Jubilee Presents: Thoughts Guided by Truth* is a print of the manuscript. We graciously appreciate your support as a foundational pillar of The House of Jubilation and look forward to the many memories and amazing experiences we will manifest together. Enjoy and express yourself as you continue to learn more about yourself on this journey of self-discovery.

With Love,

The House of Jubilation LLC Team

# Acknowledgements

This book is dedicated to all the beings on this planet who feel as though there is more to life beyond our five senses. A testament to the awareness of a metaphysical force, this archive of poems is for those focused on expanding their consciousness. May we elevate and transcend humanity's collective mind to a state of harmony and love resonance.

I would like to acknowledge the Earth, Sun, and Moon for sustaining, energizing, and stabilizing this reality. I am so thankful for the beings who co-create this existence; it is only because we are here together that any of this is possible. I am profoundly grateful for the entirety of my family and the lineage from which I stem. Special recognition goes to my mother, Mary Taylor-Richardson, and my father, Ronald Gerard Richardson. It is because of their love, union in matrimony, and sacrifices that I have been rewarded with this magnificent life in which I can create and share art.

I also profess my gratitude and appreciation for the creative community within Detroit, Michigan, and surrounding areas. It is because of these talented artists, whom I have had the pleasure to watch, work with, learn from, and befriend, that I have progressed full steam ahead on this mountainous journey as an artist with such virtue and vigor. In March of 2021, the spoken word and poetry community accepted me with open arms and held space for me to grow while discovering a self within me that I did not know existed. Some artists that I would like to recognize by name, who in particularly contributed to my development as a poet, are Hakeem the Peoples Poet; Torrey Gray, Solfull Poetry, Mila Lynn, Maya Lynn, Myna The One, Morgan Madden, Stephen McCorry, Allison Spins Ottjepka, Alexandria Kaleward, Andre Reed, Bayan the Poet, Tieler Houston, DJ Nehku, KT the Conscious Poet, Darren OV Dash, Vasgo, Siso, Mike Marriot, Bryce The Third, Hannah Larae, and Brooklyn Soleil. A special thanks is given to Devon Yancy, Rodrick Scott Jr. & Sevan Bomar's Sibyl for their contribution towards crafting the artwork for this book. There are many other great artists with whom I have had the honor of growing up alongside. I look forward to the creation of many more magnificent moments with all these creatives with whom the stars have aligned for us to come together! I ask that all praise, admiration, and glory be given to The Most High!

# Synopsis

### *A Full Circle*
A meditation on life's cyclical nature, exploring the intricate dance of beginnings and endings, and the wisdom gathered through each revolution.

### *Free Mind*
A self-questioning of mental liberation, delving into the empowerment and clarity that arises from unshackled thoughts and unbounded perspectives.

### *Guide Us Home*
A heartfelt plea for guidance and direction, invoking a deep yearning for a return to one's true essence and sanctuary.

### *Something You Imagined*
A contemplative journey into the realm of dreams, questioning the blurred lines between reality and imagination.

***Treasured Chest***
An exploration of invaluable memories and emotions, safeguarded within the heart's intimate vault.

***Behind The Wheel***
A journey into the driver's seat of life, innerstanding control, direction, and the roads we choose.

***Imagine It to Be***
A delve into the power of feeling and the creative force of our imagination in shaping reality.

***No Longer Waiting***
A declaration of proactive agency, breaking free from stagnation and seizing the moment.

***Drop of the Sea***
A reflection on individual significance within the vastness of existence.

***Thinking of You***
An intimate rumination on the enduring presence of a cherished one in the mind.

***Lullaby***
A soothing serenade that evokes a sense of peace and nostalgic comfort.

### Like A Phoenix
A tale of resurgence and rebirth, mirroring the mythical bird's cyclical transformation.

### Until Sparks Fly
A contemplation on reigniting passion, emphasizing the transient nature of feelings.

### Organized Chaos
Delves into the intricacies of structured disorder, illustrating life's unpredictable yet patterned flow.

### Walk With Self
A tale of introspection and self-awareness, emphasizing the importance of inner companionship.

### I Am Already There
A profound realization of one's presence in moments, highlighting the essence of now.

### Straight Path
A quest of steadfastness and unwavering determination, even amidst life's twists and turns.

### Resonance of Eternity
A meditative dive into timelessness, emphasizing the endless echoes of existence.

### Go - Rest | Speak - Listen: Balanced Rhythms
An analysis on balance, the importance of innerstanding timing, and the patterns of existence.

### Inner Wonders: A Testament to Miracles
A celebration of life's innate magic and the profound wonders within oneself.

### Meant to Be
An affirmation of destiny and the abundance of the Earth, emphasizing contentment with the present.

### Summer's Enlightenment
An encouragement to embrace the present and marvel at life's evanescent mysteries.

### On The Scale
A testament to universal balance and the intricate connections that form life's tapestry.

### Journey of Rediscovery
An ode to self-growth, the importance of self-focus, and recognizing the value within.

**Resonance of OM**
A rumination of the profound power of the sacred sound and its alignment with one's inner self.

**Voice of an Angel**
A whimsical interaction with a sparrow, symbolizing guidance towards freedom and elevation.

**Honored Abode**
A transcendent journey through spiritual realms, emphasizing honor and the joy of awakening.

**My Space (Tender Love & Care)**
A proclamation of self-love, innerstanding one's divine origins, and the importance of self-care.

**Product of You**
A purposeful dive into self-realization, interconnectedness, and innerstanding one's place in the world.

**Entire Book**
A reflection on one's journey of life, likened to the chapters of a continuously evolving book.

***Reflection***
An interactive space for readers to chronicle their thoughts and emotions after engaging with the poems.

# A Full Circle

It is here where I have chosen to begin!

Underneath the Golden Tree of Time,

One can learn that one can live without limits.

Trapped between the small and big hands of the Clock is a gem.

It only appears at 2:30 when Sol is hovering over tides,

Only those who believe can see the message.

Gently tapped on my pineal by a feather,

I was ushered to the moon.

It was a crescent that pointed me to a temple placed before the gates.

After a walk initiated by thoughts guided by truth, I reached the portal.

The grand gateway, an entrance leading within the clouds, veiling a supreme consciousness.

At first, I was struck by awe when I discovered all things are possible,

A notion that reminded me of everything, everywhere, all at once.

A full circle.

Once I zoomed out to breathe in another perspective,

I saw that the circle never ends... It is here where I have chosen to begin

# Free Mind

What is The Unknown to someone

Who realizes that all they know

Began as unfamiliar?

How mysterious could something be?

When everything in this world has at least one thing in common.

It is not me,

Or at least what I perceive myself to be.

To proceed into Thee,

As being birthed into... see?

I think sight is a peculiar sense.

I still visualize when I close my eyes...

What world does a blind man see

If all he has are his dreams?

Try to imagine the unimaginable,

What image comes to mind?

Yet still,

Thoughts absent of words

Make me feel like... everything.

An act called meditation,

Acting as my mediation

Between my flesh and essence.

Blessing my presence,

Duly anointed, disciplined by a sacred purpose,

Worthy of respect and dedication.

My emancipation? Free.

My next inhalation? Free.

My shackles unbound from a nation's crimes:

Free Mind.

I now see that you see
The true reality of being
for what it is.
Everything is a product of
you.

# Guide Us Home

I see myself deeply ingrained,

Like magic seeds embedded into the crust of the Earth.

I have visions of being constantly watered by your senses,

Till I sprout like the beanstalk, growing past the clouds.

Soon, it will be time for you to climb.

You will not fall like a wobbling giant,

For you are destined to prosper...

Sweet memories that lay idle,

Born out of passion,

Deep in the mantle,

You will find molten flames of intense desire.

A powerful fuel ready to combust and energize the whole,

Sparking a flame to lead the way

And guide us home.

## Something You Imagined

My hands are full,

And I just missed a step.

So, down I go.

I failed,

Received an 'F' for this letter grade.

But this was merely a test,

A check-in,

To see if I'm conscious of where I'm at.

Where am I?

The answer to this question? I am.

Currently studying, becoming more lucid every night,

I see visions of me acing my next examination,

Leading me to relocate my class

To one where all that surrounds me speaks of abundance and growth.

I am free to roam amongst the stars within this womb,

Those incubating the light and concealing the darkness within.

I am sprouting seeds of faith in the garden of my mind,

Now bearing cornucopias in multitude.

I have received my metaphysical wings,

Carrying me to heights

My former self would not believe exist.

Yet here I am, seeing that they do.

Proof is in the experience of sensation.

What have you seen in the last 24 hours that made you feel?

Was it real?

Or is everything something you imagined?

# Treasured Chest

Blackened clouds of smog

Obscure the heir of Earth's gifts,

Clouding their vision densely like fog.

In your darkest hour,

The illusion will pass.

Truth arises at last.

But first,

You face the reflection of the cumulative

Amount of fault you have yearned for.

You will see all of sin for what it truly is:

A mistake to be corrected, punishment is unnecessary.

You might not have cast a stone,

But surely, one was in hand.

Instead of judging yourself and others:

Band your organs together,

Organize the organisms that perpetuate your life,

And take account of your actions.

Look into yourself and see why you are who you are.

Choose to be accountable for yourself,

No longer yielding to false authorities

That claims to govern your existence.

And in that instance,

You might feel loss like never before.

Things that are bad for you

Can be hard to let go of.

And in that moment,

Feeling lost might be overwhelming,

Because you have never known true freedom.

Worry not about things out of your control.

Though many, still ensnared in society's fiery spell,

Might try to convince you that you are misled,

Remember:

Before the smoke clears, The Most High will navigate you through the fog.

Know that true victory lies in inner control.

Relaxed and alert,

Breathe in the champion's breath,

A precious gift from the Earth,

Added to your treasured chest.

# Behind The Wheel

Imagine you, a passive controller,

Speak of information derived from wisdom.

Makes remarks akin to that of a backseat driver,

Speaking heavily upon what you think one should do.

Feeling as if that is the best possible action for one to take,

And it is what would happen if they were you.

You love the challenge of solving a good puzzle,

So, you consider yourself helping those nearest,

By dropping a clue.

This may seem fulfilling at the moment,

Adventurous and thrilling,

Because of the way you magically make people feel.

Yet still, not knowing that continuing in this way,

Will unravel the dream we consider real.

You might wonder why what you do affects others so greatly.

You change reality for others,

Because you are the one behind the wheel,

Sealed into position like that of a seam.

As a coachman,

You are here to safely guide your vehicle with focus,

To the agreed-upon designated destination.

Not to micromanage the passengers which incarnate your ship.

This is a journey for the sake of travel,

Not a matter of racing.

Steer your mind away from the chaos of sporadic thoughts,

Because if you do not,

Everyone will be lost.

## Imagine It to Be

Lately, I have been a dreamer,

Deeply ingrained in the visions of the mind.

So much so, it has become equivalent

To the physical world I use to consider "reality."

Sometimes I find myself walking through life,

Having vivid recollection of my dreams as if they happened here;

But I guess, in a way, they did.

Events occurring in the form of thoughts in my head.

Maybe that's all life ever was?

Even when I interact with someone in this physical plane of existence,

I am merely left with memories of those experiences;

Which are only real in my head.

See,

I may have some thought of what was said,

But it's possible the other feels as though it happened differently.

Instead,

They have an entirely unique set of remembrances

Of those precious moments we shared together.

Whether it happened the way I thought or not,

What I think to be so...

Is so,

For me.

So, I ask,

What is reality?

And I answer myself... It is whatever you imagine it to be.

# No Longer Waiting

Through the peephole I can see

A being, housing the energy of artistic passion and expression,

Approaching in the distance.
They spark a feeling.

Nerves propelled this sensation,
Aflutter, traversing through this body like butterflies.

It's this feeling in my bones that got me moving like, lightning!
Cautiously, step by step, absent of haste,
I opened the door to the unknown.

I did not expect to see anything of familiarity,
But here, standing in front of me,
Not even three feet away,
Was the young person known for their exceptional skills.

A person whom I knew only through a past variation
Of the self I call "me"...
They said to me,
"I am waiting on you."

Deep down inside, I knew why.
It was also mentioned that they "have my number",

Signaling that a connection is there,
A direct line, capable of going two ways.

But I know,
I am the one who needs to make the first call,
Ringing into fruition the real,
Pulled out of the sea of illusion and its dark depths.

I accept the path of this quest.
It is time to tread a course of a magnificent journey,
Previously only privy to the imagination.
I decide to act now,
No longer waiting.

# Drop of the Sea

Just a momentary thought of you
Brings me solace, draws me to a home anew.
Heavy rain shattering the façade,
The illusion wherein I had been awed.

Reign blown out of proportion,
People extol your magnificence with distortion.
"Rain, rain, go away,"
Some might wishfully say.

But I see your truth, your core so stark,
A life's renewal, an ever-flowing spark.
Here you are, here you will stay,
Your essence will not just drift away.

A maze meant

To be loved by patient and unconditional energy

In which innerstands you are not a puzzle to be solved,

But a force of nature, ever evolved.

May I witness, may I perceive,
Your electrifying existence, the myths you weave.

Like lightning, grounded yet free,
Neither here nor there, your power surrounds me like air.

In an instant, in a snap,
I'm enveloped, I am struck by awe.
A wonder meant to baffle, to enthrall.

You are inspiration, the world's driving force,
The very essence that sets life on its course.
Even if you were to love in reverse,
In your presence, my spirit would still traverse.

Like butterflies, your essence takes flight,
Signifying change, and nature's sheer might.
Life's elixir, so profound and true,
A drink of the gods, forever renewing the blue.

# Thinking of You

Much of my time is dedicated to
thinking of you.
I'm not sure if you are thinking of me,
too,
But sometimes, it feels as though you
are.

You come to mind when I speak of
random things,
And when I close my eyes, your image
still clings.
In dreams, you appear, in scenes so
vast,
Extravagant as blockbusters with
budgets for an all-star cast.
I cherish every moment, every subtle
jest,
Whether you are the leading actress
or just a guest.

Your presence radiates, iridescent in
its glow;
Though miles apart, in my mind, you
are close.
Close to my Anahata Chakra, you are
near and dear.
My heart beats passionately,
shedding every fear.

When I look into your eyes, serenity I find:
Calmness, balance, a connection of a kind.
I feel unhurt, unbeaten, and unbowed,
Yet with every greeting, a humble namaste I have vowed.

To stay with you, alone, for endless time,
Is to connect with the Divine so sublime.
For it is you, always you, who is forever on my mind.

# Lullaby

My lullaby calls to me,
Singing melodies in sync with nature's vibration.
Coordination as graceful as lily pads landing on a pond,
Here is rejuvenation in its purest form.

Water is present, offering tranquility in its flow,
And the air carries the whisper of her thoughts.
In spirit, I sense the flames of her passion,
Yearning to ignite and glow.

Feasting on the fruits of the Earth,
I feel enveloped in love and nurture.
Rooted deeply in the soil,
I listen, enchanted in the sounds of my lullaby.

# Like A Phoenix

A gust of burning flames
Fills my heart's chambers,
Igniting overwhelming passion.
It produces heat—
A fervent energy.

Moisture in the air
Meets this blaze,
And together they birth steam.
It feels as if time has paused.
Is this the essence of bliss?

Your lips, so close to mine,
Pull me into the gravity of a pending kiss.
Happiness envelopes me in your presence,
Joy floods me at the thought of you.

Warm like hot cocoa on a snow-kissed day,
You make my heart melt—
And yet, with you, it rises again.
Reborn, like a phoenix.

# Until Sparks Fly

Have you ever felt the warmth of love?
A passion that once sparked—
You blaze, a fire potent enough to
consume an entire forest.
It all began with the tiniest ember.

From within, it flourished,
Illuminating the path to endearment.
A profound affection,
Designed to bring joy to others'
hearts.

Such intimacy discovered,
A bond so luminous that even ice
melts in its presence.
Love—
Once felt, should be held in
reverence.

For, eventually, every flame will wane,
Succumbing to a mere gust of wind.
Yet, hope remains,
Until sparks fly once again.

I now see that you see
The true reality of being
for what it is.
Everything is a product of
you.
I mean, with all due
respect when it comes to
you in mind,
But yours and mine are
not that different, you
see.
I envisioned a wonderful
image of everything that
is not me
Being with me,
While I embark to discover
what it means to be me
Through experiencing you.
But I now see that you see
the true reality of being
for what it is.
Everything is a product of
you...

# Organized Chaos

Self-awareness is not for the purpose
of controlling your experiences.
The discovery of self is a continuous
journey of mindful reflection on your
feelings and tendencies.

Conduct your observations without
judgment;
There is no need to rationalize your
emotions.

You are not your thoughts.
You are not your trauma.
You are an infinite being, expressing
itself currently in a divine manner.

Give yourself grace.
This is the duality in which you feel:
Yin and Yang.

The complementary forces of the
contrary in their natural state,
Interconnected, existing in
interdependence.
One perpetuates the other, and vice
versa.

Organized Chaos.

# Walk With Self

I am raw in my passion, genuine with emotion,
An entity of energy, subtly explosive in motion.
Oscillating between the mysterious and the known,
Presenting the multifaceted nature of being, uniquely shown.

My messages, perhaps peculiar in their relay,
To you, may read in this way:
Unexplainable yet plausible,
Indefinable, but imaginable. Is it not?

You may never fully grasp the essence of my soul,
But you can sense my presence, my whole.

See you could never know me for me,

But you can sense me while I, being me, am here as I.

Do you see yourself for who you truly are? In totality? In reality?

Do you see your reflection, complete and true?
Beyond mortality's fleeting view?

Do you see past the desires and dreams of another,
In your quest to discover?

What defines your sanity?

Candidly, to be frank for a moment.

We are all in a loop,

We have done the same things over and over expecting life to change,

Fortified in it like a tank.

Ponder, reflect, think... For in a moment's blink,

You might glimpse another realm, another dimension,

A world awaiting your attentive cognition.

But if you are tethered to the mundane view,

You might dismiss this bliss, this new avenue.

A world, marvelous yet overlooked,

By those too attached to the conventional playbook.

See, look... If you feel aligned with the herd of masses who find life a bore,

It is time for introspection, time to explore.

Venture out, delve deep within your core, embark on a walk with self and you will discover so much more.

# I Am Already There

Too many times have I been down,
Walking on the lowest depths, caught between a rock and a hard place.
Trying to carve out space for a brighter me...

I envision a version of myself that reaches such heights,
When I extend my hand, I touch the cloud filled sky.
And as I look down, wings unfurled and ready,
I'm certain, without doubt, that I will fly.

Soaring beyond any plane or fabled creature known to man,
To journey through the vast expanse of air.
For in my mind, the vision is so vivid, so clear.
To me, it feels as though I am already there.

# Straight Path

Have I demanded too much from this world?
Seeking privacy amidst the crowd,
Longing for quiet, away from the loud.
Yet in the same breath, wishing to be cherished by multitudes,
While treasuring moments of solitude.

I yearn for a voice that rings clear and true,
Yet in gatherings, silence is my chosen hue.
In a world teeming with distrust and fear,
I seek love, genuineness, and truth so sincere.

Yet as I walk with faith, ever so brave,
I become acutely aware of the shadow of hate.
For what I hold dear, others may seek to plunder,
In this world of wonder and blunder.

Yet, with hope in my heart, I choose to wait,
While actively seeking the divine traits:
Patience, discernment, protection, and grace.

Even as foes reveal their guise,
I recognize the reflection of past ties.

For in a moment of disruption, I might have caused a stir,
Yet through all life's trembles and shakes,
I've held my ground, un-swayed by mistakes.

Have you ever stood firm when the ground seemed amiss?
Walking a straight path, undeterred by those who hiss?

# Resonance of Eternity

In the vast expanse of existence,
Everything resonates.

All is vibration,

Some things are faster than others.
From the subtle to the vigorous,
Each in its unique state.
Constantly moving,
Even what seems still to the eyes is always in motion.

What is it to emote?
To channel, to highlight, to denote emotions deep and remote.
Is the "E" for "Eternal"?
An everlasting notion, hinting at the timeless nature of every sentiment's footnote.

Eternal – it transcends time,
Echoes through eons, sublime.
Enduring, steadfast, and forever prevailing,
Its essence never fading, never failing.
For eternity is not just about age,
It's the undying spirit, an unending stage.

Eternal means perpetual,
A cycle that is continuous and sequential.
Though we may begin and end in time's flow,
Our essence, our frequency, will eternally glow.
Rebirthed, reimagined, rejuvenated,
Time and time again, perpetually celebrated, there is no true end.

## Go – Rest | Speak – Listen: Balanced Rhythms

Wait your turn.

Everything flows smoothly when acted upon accordingly.

Learn the placements of order.

There is a time to go,

And another to rest.

Oscillation occurs between the two.

For us, binary digits serve as clues.

The zeros & ones that create a multitude of options to choose.

There is a moment to speak, and another to listen.

*Sign & print your name here if you truly bear witness:*

Print:_____
Signature:_____
Date_____

# Inner Wonders: A Testament to Miracles

If ever you seek a sign beyond yourself,
Look here and see the proof of miracles.
Pause. Take this time
To inhale deeply and then slowly release.
There is no need to ask; no permission is required
To breathe, to live, to exist.
In this moment, innerstand that you are the "wonder."
Cheers to our connection, a testament to cosmic synchronicity.
Life is not a challenge to overcome; it is a dream, living what we chose to become.
Images and feelings we constantly craft,
The universe moves with each breath and laugh.
Within every pulse of life, the Divine lives.

All we need to do is listen, trust, and believe in what we find inside.

What we envision, our deepest desires, with patience, action, & faith, will manifest and raise us higher.

# Meant to Be: "Destined Journey"

You are exactly where you are meant to be.
Can you see the abundance which Earth has provided for you?
A special place for you to grow and flourish.
A space nourishing the varied aspects that makes you,

The you that we know you to be.

My beloved,
It's not about getting the most.
Be wary of those who boast.
It's about cherishing what you hold close.
When you open your eyes to what you have been endowed with,
You'll discern your path.

This is the same journey you have walked since the beginning.
When you remember, this is the way you chose; you are winning.
As long as you continue to move straight forward,
You are amongst the living.
This is the way.
It is meant to be.

# Summer's Enlightenment

I urge you to become comfortable with the unknown.

Those moments which you may believe to be strange.

It all begins with realizing your senses have limited range.

You and the other may not be on the same page.

But that difference makes no difference.

When you add into account that once y'all both move on,

That which was previously experienced is now gone.

Be wary of those whose minds lay idle in the realm of the past,

Exploring their previously traversed thoughts as vast.

Casting visions upon today,

By memories that have long since faded away.

Wow!

Amazement is an expression that someone could never be if they feel as though they know it all.

When bearing the beams of summer's enlightenment turns into fall.

# On The Scale

Immersed in creativity's spirit,
An exuberant soul you will find,
Radiating love and gratitude
passionately
For Earth and all creations of The
Great Mother combined.

We all fit as pieces in a cosmic puzzle,
A realm of interdependence,
A world that knows coexistence's
function:
Balance and harmony.

On the scale, they place:
A feather
And humanity's heart, so free.
If unity escapes our embrace,
What a tragic calamity it would be.

Yet, if we prevail,
Boundless magnificence upon us will
replete.

In due time, during the day of
Judgement, we will see.

# Journey of Rediscovery

For every person I believed had forgotten me,

A thousand others reminded me they remembered.

As I evolved,

Some facets of myself became obsolete.

It was beyond time to let go;

I clung on merely because past emotions felt genuine and strong.

But my future was poised to usher me into the new,

Limiting my relations to a chosen few,

And a voice that whispered, "focus on you."

When I gaze into the mirror;

I see a vision of love and grandeur,

A smile acknowledging my resilience and fortitude,

A hearty laugh, realizing the gift of life,

Eyes shimmering with ambition and future strides.

Now, I embark on an inward quest,

A path of realignment.

A journey of rediscovery.

# Resonance of OM

Utter the word,

The magic one...

It sets the tone,

OM...

A resonance spanning time's expanse,

From start to finish, it holds a stance.

This sound,

Will reign supreme,

If words hold true,

And actions align with what we say.

Live beyond mere thought's array,

For you are more than the mind's fray.

Within, you will find,

All you have ever looked for and needed.

The truth of reality is in your core,
rooted and deeply seeded.

## **Voice of an Angel**

In my ear, I hear the chirping of a bird,

Not just any winged being,

But my favorite one: a sparrow.

Every time I would go out to cut grass,

One would fly a circuit around me,

Always moving at such a fast pace:

Zoom. Swoosh.

As it passed me by,

I would ponder why

It chose to circle just me.

I loved hearing its chirps which began to sound like words.

In my ear, I would then discern, "Follow me! Follow me!"

I would lift my gaze to the sky,

And there, yet again, was the sparrow.

That twittering sound,

Always the voice of an angel,

Joyfully singing, "Follow me! Follow me!"

In that instance, I realized, to follow those with wings is the path to freedom.

# Honored Abode

As my soul traversed the realm of the Astral Plane,

Making way to my body in only a hair of a second,

The symbol "honor" was uttered, filling my dome completely.

Stimulated from the vibrations of such a powerful sound,

Immediately, my nostrils took in a gust of cool air.

Prāna, moving through my canals, provided the necessary energy

For my spirit to animate my vessel.

Arose I did, in a state of bliss.

I felt the sensation of being absent from the clutter of thoughts.

This joy continued as brightness blanketed my receptors of light.

I gazed upon a most magnificent, fluorescent, multi-colored dragon,

I named this entity Bloom.

This ineffable being continues to remind me that I can fly.

So, every rising, I spring out of my comfortable bed with exuberance,

Whether amidst the waves of heat or the flakes of snow.

The degree of hot versus the degree of cold,

Oh yes, I feel so bold.

I completed my first task for the day inside my room with a smile,

I am happily ready to interact with grace inside of my honored abode.

# My Space "Tender Love & Care"

I woke up this rising,

And for the first time,

I chose myself.

Today I needed some

Mind Space.

A little TLC to my-self,

For my Mental Health.

I woke up this Rising,

And this time,

I chose myself.

No longer waiting for the rays of the most passionate being I know

To show me how to glow,

How to Gloat!

Isn't that what it means to be the G.O.A.T.?

The greatest of all time they say.

Isn't it quite humorous

To know?

To know what,

You might ask?

To know that the path that

You claim to own

Is led by the lux of another.

And the road you are on always has been,

And always will be if you do not see.

Seize this opportunity is what they will tell you.

Seas of ops per every tune,

I cross my t's, and dot my I's

Trying to get this message of unity of hue,

To you Hakeem.

A powerful messenger of the light indeed,

Showed me that my seed

Not only come from kings and queens but also gods and goddesses.

So wouldn't that mean GOD exists

Through what is called ME?

But I am just a mere reflection of everything.

So, I guess all of this is Omni,

On Me.

Aware of my current self-realization,

I woke up this Rising,

And for the first time,

I chose myself.

Just a little Tender Love & Care to
Myself for my Mental Health,

My Space.

# Product of You

I now see that you see
The true reality of being for what it is.
Everything is a product of you.
I mean, with all due respect when it comes to you in mind,
But yours and mine are not that different, you see.
I envisioned a wonderful image of everything that is not me
Being with me,
While I embark to discover what it means to be me
Through experiencing you.
But I now see that you see the true reality of being for what it is.
Everything is a product of you,
And I just exist within it.
I mean, eyes exist within it,
Because you are my foresight and clarity.
Without you,
I would be ignorant,
Waiting for flint to spark my passion again.
I never thought about visiting Rio when I was young,
But as soon as my aspirations of going to places I never seen before,
Like Portugal and Brazil,

Current had become solid, as if steel...

As if still,

The King of all viruses was alive to remind me that the bars placed on our Ancestors are still very real.

Heal?

Some say the hills have eyes,
And I ask,
What do they see?
Because whatever higher point of view they have must be fogged by the clouds of sky.
Pressing play now, no rewind.
So, I can see now in real time
The wisdom of those in which I will refer to for the sake of privacy as "Cavemen,"
Or now commonly known as "Mountain Men."
I mean, they mounted men in a solidified position which made men cave in.

By chance,
Do you know a fellow with a Man Cave? Or wish they had one?
A special place to be Bruce for a day:

Almighty or Wayne?
Either way it goes,
They're both _____.
I mean, right,
You can do whatever you want to do.

So why not produce?
Indeed, planting a seed is more
fruitful than burning up some weed.
Weave through the nonsense,
I mean that which none sense.
Because if nine senses you,
It's safe to say that you make sense.
And if you are sensible, indeed,
You may now see,
That I now see,
That you see the true reality of being
for what it is.
Everything is a product of you.

# Entire Book

I see an image of the person I aspire to become,

Witnessing my ever-changing form,

A continuous rebirthing I undergo.

Throughout time, glimpses of my ideal self-appear,

Traits radiant and profound,

Yet never fully present in a single bound.

Fragments of my desired self are lost in past deeds.

As time advances, my memories endure,

A fact I cherish with delight.

For the facets of the perfect me are not mere fantasies,

But phases I have navigated,

Like diverse chapters in a narrative.

Though each segment varies,

They are still interwoven, and it is
this connection that crafts my tale—

An entire book of the path I have
chosen to spell.

# Dear Honored Reader,

Thank You for making it this far, I am so appreciative and grateful for your presence. It means the world to me, to be able to share some of my most sacred inner thoughts with you. Reading these poems humor me, because each poem takes me to the moment I was in while writing them. In this way Art is truly a time capsule, transcending the bounds of space and time. Every single last one of these poems helped me in a time of need, whether it was expressing pent up emotions for another or feeling lost in this world just trying to figure out why I am here & where I am going and everything else in between. It is my desire that this archive helps others in the way in which it helped me, so feel free to share this book with anyone who you feel may receive help from one of these messages. Before we part ways, I want you to know that I am proud of you, and I know that you are shining your light amongst the world in a magnificent way. Remember none of this would exist without you. YOU MATTER, DON'T EVER FORGET HOW IMPORTANT YOU ARE! In the following pages you will find a section dedicated to YOU. This final part of

Reuel Jubilee Presents: *Thoughts Guided by Truth* is meant for you to reflect in any way you consider necessary, this is your book, and you are the author of your journey...

Sincerely,

Reu'el Richardson

# YOU MAY NOW COMMENCE

# Reflection

*This section is dedicated to YOU and YOUR thoughts*

_____
_____
_____
_____
_____
_____
_____
_____
_____
_____
_____
_____
_____
_____
_____
_____
_____
_____
_____
_____
_____
_____
_____
_____
_____

*Reuel Jubilee presents:*

# Thoughts Guided by Truth

*Poetry to aid you along your spiritual journey through the collective mind.*

www.ingramcontent.com/pod-product-compliance
Lightning Source LLC
Chambersburg PA
CBHW020807160426
43192CB00006B/473